ANCESTOR'S CALL

With a Reprint of the Slave Narrative:
Narrative of the Life of Moses Grandy; Late a Slave
In the United States of America
(1843 London, England Edition)

By
Eric Anthony Sheppard

Published by:
Tech-Rep Associates, Inc.
P.O. Box 8046
Elkridge, Maryland 21075

Special Thanks:

I would like to take the opportunity to thank the Creator of us all for allowing me to share this information. I also want to thank my wife, Lisa, for her support and encouragement in writing this book. Through all the long hours of research and travel, you supported my efforts and helped to keep me focused. In countless ways you have contributed directly to the publishing efforts of this book. I appreciate you and all that you have done. We are not finished, and it's only just begun. I love you!

Contents

ANCESTOR'S CALL

INTRODUCTION

It is wonderful when a project becomes a mission in your life. That is exactly what has happened for me in writing this book. I have been purchasing books on writing novels and screenplays for at least fifteen years. Something in me just kept revisiting this faint passion as time went by. Well, the passion has blossomed into commitment.

I have committed my time and energy to go along with the talents and skills given to me by Yahweh (God) to write this book and continue forward the legacy of one of my ancestors, Moses Grandy. A faint passion of mine to some day write a book or screenplay has now turned into a burning desire to finish this project and search for additional stories within my own ancestry.

I wish that I could attribute this burning desire to write to an exceptional learned talent of mine. That however is not the case. I believe this is a gift from the Almighty Creator, not only to allow me to exercise my creative skills, but to also fulfill a mission that started over two hundred years ago.

About six years ago I began on a journey of self-identification. My quest was not to change my name to a more afro-centric one, but to research my ancestry and determine my heritage. I was blessed to discover many relatives and friends that before this point in my life I did not know. During my research I found information on one of my ancestors that immediately gave me the answer to one of my missions in life. Moses Grandy's quest for freedom of his relatives was a continual process. I plan to continue this process. Consequently, the once faint passion to write this book is now the burning flame of freedom for me.

This book is dedicated to my ancestors and the people that helped in various ways to support my efforts. Without the many sacrifices and shear determination of Moses Grandy, this book would not be possible. The University of North Carolina Libraries at Chapel Hill should also be commended for their vision to provide electronic versions of many slave narratives in their *"Documenting the American South"* Collection.

I appreciate the assistance given to me by many individuals that work at the local, state and federal institutions which house vital statistics records that bring the untold past to the present. This experience has changed my life and those of my descendants forever. It is my desire that this book also serve as a beacon of encouragement for others to research their ancestry and uncover the wonderful stories of historical significance for our present and future generations.

Eric Anthony Sheppard

Chapter 1

THE PASSION WITHIN

In almost every phase of life from childhood to adulthood there are moments of truth. The question is, "how do we deal with these moments of truth?" Do we face them head on and make adjustments in our lives or do we ignore them and do nothing? I have decided to meet the challenges and search for the truth of my past.

I do not believe for one minute that I alone was totally responsible for coming to this point in my life. My ancestors have left the spirit of their courage, talents, ingenuity, and faith for me to carry forward and make this world a better place to live.

All of us have a responsibility to explore our purpose for living. Our purpose should make a positive contribution to our families and the society in which we live. I strongly believe that knowing your ancestral past can help improve your chances for making a positive contribution to the world. I came to this conclusion by examining my own life experiences and observing the lives of others.

I sincerely hope that the information that I share in this book serves as a catalyst to heal the hurt and pain of some individuals, as well as this country, by researching our American history that has the tree-rotted roots of slavery in its past.

During my research I came upon a quote by a R.D.W. Conner that states, "No people who are indifferent to their past need hope to make their future great". If we as descendents of African-American ancestry ever hope to achieve greatness as a people, we must embrace our past that includes the positive and negative aspects of our history.

My journey to arrive at this point in my life is no chance happening, accident, or mistake. The passion to research and write this book may have been a direct result of the trails blazed by my ancestors many centuries ago. My research guided me to an ancestor's narrative that was written in 1843. That ancestor, Moses Grandy, left a legacy of information and history. My desire is to carry the torch during my generation and past it on to my descendents and relatives.

I started researching my family ancestry soon after the events of the Million Man March in October 1995. The experience of participating in such a momentous event and being associated with black people of such different schools of thought was one of those moments of truth I described earlier. After that experience, I felt as though I did not belong with any of those schools of thought. I had my own ideas and wanted to express them.

The Million Man March was a historically significant event in American history. The magnitude of the cooperation expressed by those that helped to plan and organized the event was amazing in itself. I shall be forever grateful to have participated in that event because it allowed me to examine myself and determine where I fit in the world picture.

I knew instinctively how some fellow marchers did not think I measured up to some of the Afro-centric, religious, and fraternal organizational methodologies that were present during the planning efforts. To be truthful, there were times that I thought I did not measure up. I have come to learn however that all of those emotions were necessary in order for me to get to the point of researching my own ancestry.

Discovering the narrative written by Moses Grandy was truly a liberating experience for me. Through his Narrative, I discovered my ancestors were as much a part of the struggle for freedom as anyone else. All of us have a right to claim and continue the legacy of our forefathers in whatever capacity allowed.

Regardless of your station in life, we all have a roll to play in making the society and country we live in better. After reading the Moses Grandy slave narrative in Chapter Two, I sincerely hope that many who read this book come to the same conclusion.

All of us should have a Million Man March event in their life. What is yours? What is the significant emotional event in your life that stimulates your passion for searching for the truth in your life? I had to look back in order to move forward.

I wanted to know something about my father's relatives since I basically grew up mostly interacting with my mother's family. I did know my paternal grandmother (Elnora Grandy Sheppard) and I had the opportunity to share some quality time with her in my youth. But, with the exception of her sister, Mary Grandy Jackson, and a few cousins, I did not know the rest of the Grandy family living in Baltimore, Maryland and around the country.

The concept of this book is not to outline the genealogy of the Grandy family, but to demonstrate the relevancy of African-American history in the United States and break the yoke of guilt and shame felt by descendents of slaves in America when confronted with our past.

After reading the slave narrative, I could never be ashamed or feel guilty of my ancestors' past. The Grandys were blessed by Moses Grandy to have been left a documented trail of reference for future generations. The Grandys were but one-fourth of the ancestral linage. The blessing was passed on to any of my ancestors that endured the horrors of slavery.

I can trace my great-great grandfather, Edmond[1] Grandy, to the location and community in which most of the slave narrative's story takes place. A system existed in that era of American history to destroy the ancestral knowledge and records of my blood relations. I will not allow the practices of slave owners to define my heritage. If they tried to take my heritage away from me, it would be foolish to let them have an ounce of validity in the research process I use to re-establish my heritage or choose my ancestry.

Therefore, I consider all the slaves and their relatives from the Courthouse Township area of Camden County, North Carolina my ancestors and/or relatives. There are some things not found in documents, but can be located in your soul. I am inspired and called by my ancestors to continue the progress made by Moses Grandy 160 years ago through my research efforts and by writing this book.

As a passion and mission for my life, I have decided to research the Grandy family links originating from Camden, North Carolina and other descendants of families mentioned in the narrative. This is no small task, and one that may take generations to accomplish. But just as the torch has been passed to me, the ancestors will call others to carry on the work that was started decades ago.

---

[1] My great-great grandfather's first name has been legally recorded as both "Edmond" and "Edmund". For this book, I have used the "Edmond" spelling.

In Chapter 2, is the original 1843 version of the slave narrative I read from the *Documenting the American South* Collection digitization format located at the University of North Carolina Libraries at Chapel Hill. During my research, I also came across an 1844 version of the narrative printed in Boston, Massachusetts that is part of the Eisenhower Rare Book Collection at Johns Hopkins University in Baltimore, Maryland. There are some slight differences in the 1844 version that I will elaborate on more thoroughly in Chapter 3.

This story, without a doubt, has touched my life in a positive way. After reading the narrative, my feelings have covered the full spectrum of human emotions. I felt honored to have an ancestor that left an important American history document that is available for us to read and study in this generation and beyond.

I felt anger at those persons who used their authority and resources to commit crimes of horrific acts against enslaved persons. Yet, there is a proud feeling I get every time I think of how Moses Grandy was so thoroughly committed to obtaining the freedom for his family and his relatives. He did not give up his dream of rescuing as many family members as he could during his lifetime.

When I read how industrious Moses Grandy was with the restrictions of slavery surrounding him, I feel like most people of today have a long way to go. We accomplish so little with the relative freedom we now enjoy. I believe that Moses is one of the many unsung heroes of the slavery era.

I strongly encourage all of us, regardless of our ethnic origin, to tell our ancestral stories to the world. They deserve to have their deeds and sacrifices recognized as well as those persons with more familiar names we have become accustomed to hearing and studying in our history over the years.

It is our responsibility to make their legacies a living reality. I indeed hope that this book will enlighten many and provide a measure of healing history and truth for those individuals willing to seek freedom for themselves.

Chapter 2

Narrative of the Life of Moses Grandy; Late a Slave in the United States of America
(1843 London, England Edition)

INTRODUCTION

ABOUT a fortnight ago, the subject of the following brief Memoir came to me, bearing with him a letter from a dear friend and distinguished abolitionist in the United States, from which the following, is an extract: "I seize my pen in haste to gratify a most worthy coloured friend of mine, by giving him a letter of introduction to you, as he intends sailing this week (August 8th, 1842,) for Liverpool and London, via New Orleans. His name is Moses Grandy. He knows what it is to have been a slave, and what are the tender mercies of the southern slave-drivers. His history is not only authentic, but most extraordinary, and full of thrilling interest. Could it published; it would make a deep sensation in every quarter. He was compelled to buy his freedom *three times over!* He paid for it 1850 dollars (nearly £400 sterling). He has since bought his wife, and one or two of his children; and before going, to England will first go to New Orleans, to purchase some of his other children if he can find them, who are still in captivity. His benevolence, affection, kindness of heart, and elasticity of spirit are truly remarkable. He has a good head, a fine countenance, and a great spirit, notwithstanding his education has been obtained in the horrible school of slavery. Just get him to tell you his narrative, and if you happen to have an Anti-slavery Meeting, let him tell his tale to a British audience." In the letter of another highly esteemed friend, he is spoken of as "unsurpassed for faithfulness and perseverance." In the letter of a third, as "a worthy and respectable man." On examining a book containing a list of the donations made him by American friends, in aid of his noble design to rescue from the miseries of slavery his relations, I found the names and certificates of persons of the highest respectability. It will be amply sufficient with those who are acquainted with the abolitionists of the United States, for me to name General Fessenden, and Nathan Winslow, Esq., of Portland, Maine; the Rev. A.A. Phelphs, Ellis Gray Loring, and Samuel E. Sewall, Esqs. of Boston, Massachusetts. Being satisfied, by these indubitable vouches, of Moses Grandy's title to credit, I listened to his artless tale with entire confidence, and with a feeling of interest which all will participate, who peruse the following pages. Considering, his narrative calculated to promote a more extensive knowledge of the workings of American slavery, and that its sale might contribute to the object which engages so entirely the mind of Moses, namely, the redemption of those who are in bonds, belonging to his family, I resolved to commit it to press, as nearly as possible in the language of Moses himself. I have carefully abstained from casting in a single reflection or animadversion of my own. I leave the touching story of the self-liberated captive to speak for itself; and the wish of my heart will be gratified, and my humble effort on his behalf be richly rewarded, if this little book be the means of obtaining for my coloured brother the assistance which he seeks, or of increasing the zeal of those who are associated for the purpose of "breaking every yoke, and setting the oppressed free."

George Thompson
9, Blandford-Place, Regent's Park,
October 18th, 1842

LIFE OF MOSES GRANDY.

MY name is Moses Grandy. I was born in Camden County, North Carolina. I believe I am fifty-six years old. Slaves seldom know exactly how old they are: Neither they nor their masters set down the time of a birth: The slaves, because they are not allowed to write or read, and the masters, because they only care to know what slaves belong to them.

The master, Billy Grandy, whose slave I was born, was a hard-drinking man: he sold away many slaves. I remember four sisters and four brothers; my mother had more children, but they were dead or sold away before I can remember. I was the youngest. I remember well my mother often hid us all in the woods, to prevent master selling us. When we wanted water, she sought for it in any hole or puddle formed by falling trees or otherwise: it was often full of tadpoles and insects: she strained it, and gave it round to each of us in the hollow of her hand. For food, she gathered berries in the woods, got potatoes, raw corn, &c. After a time the master would send word to her to come in, promising, he would not sell us. But at length persons came who agreed to give the prices he set on us. His wife, with much to be done, prevailed on him not to sell me; but he sold my brother, who was a little boy. My mother, frantic with grief, resisted their taking her child away: she was beaten and held down : she fainted; and when she came to herself, her boy was gone. She made much outcry, for which the master tied her up to a peach tree in the yard, and flogged her.

Another of my brothers was sold to Mr. Tyler, Dewan's Neck, Pasquotank County; this man very much ill-treated many coloured boys. One very cold day he sent my brother out, naked and hungry, to find a yoke of steers: the boy returned without finding them, when his master flogged him, and sent him out again; a white lady who lived near, gave him food, and advised him to try again: he did so, but it seems again without success. He piled up a heap of leaves, and laid himself down in them, and died there. He was found through a flock of turkey buzzards hovering over him; these birds had pulled his eyes out.

My young master and I used to play together; there was but two days' difference in our ages. My old master always said he would give me to him. When he died, all the coloured people were divided amongst his children, and I fell to young master; his name was James Grandy. I was then about eight years old. When I became old enough to be taken away from my mother and put to field-work, I was hired out for the year, by auction, at the Court House, every January; this is the common practice with respect to slaves belonging to persons who are under age. This continued till my master and myself were twenty-one years old.

The first who hired me was Mr. Kemp, who used me pretty Well; he gave me plenty to eat and sufficient clothing.

The next was old Jemmy Coates, a severe man. Because I could not learn his way of hilling corn, he flogged me naked with a severe whip made of a very tough sapling; this lapped round me at each stroke, the point of it at last entered my belly and broke off; leaving an inch and a-half outside. I was not aware of it until on going to work again it hurt my side very much, when on looking down I saw it sticking, out of my body: I pulled it out and the blood spouted after it. The wound festered, and discharged very much at the time, and hurt me for years after.

In being hired out, sometimes the slave gets a good home, and sometimes a bad one: when he gets a good one, he dreads to see January come; when he has a bad one, the year seems five times as long as it is.

I was next with Mr. Enoch Sawyer of Camden county: my business was to keep ferry, and do other odd work. It was cruel living; we had not near enough of either victuals or clothes; I was half-starved for half my time. I have often ground the husks of Indian corn over again in a hand-mill, for the chance of getting something to eat out of it, which the former grinding had left. In severe frosts, I was compelled to go into the fields and woods to work, with my naked feet cracked and bleeding from extreme cold: to warm them, I used to rouse an ox or hog, and stand on the place where it had lain. I was at that place three years, and very long years they seemed to me. The trick by which he kept me so long was this: -- the Court House was but a mile off; on hiring day, he prevented me from going till he went himself and bid for me. On the last occasion, he was detained for a little while by other business, so I ran as quickly as I could, and got hired before he came up.

Mr. George Furley was my next master; he employed me as a car-boy in the Dismal swamp; I had to drive lumber, &. I had plenty to eat and plenty of clothes. I was so overjoyed at the change, that I then thought I would not have left the place to go to heaven.

Next year I was hired by Mr. John Micheau of the same county, who married my young mistress, one of the daughters of Mr. Grandy, and sister to my present owner. This master gave us very few clothes, and but little to eat; I was almost naked. One day he came into the field, and asked why no more work was done. The older people were afraid of him; so I said that the reason was, we were so hungry, we could not work. He went home and told the mistress to give us plenty to eat, and at dinner time we had plenty. We came out shouting for joy, and went to work with delight. From that time, we had food enough, and he soon found that he had a great deal more work done. The field was quite alive with the people striving who should do most.

He hired me for another year. He was a great gambler; He kept me up five nights together, without sleep night or day, to wait on the gambling table. I was standing in the corner of the room, nodding for want of sleep,

when he took up the shovel, and beat me with it: he dislocated my shoulder, and sprained my wrist, and broke the shovel over me. I ran away, and got another person to hire me.

This person was Mr. Richard Furley, who after that hired me at the Court House every year, till my master came of age. He gave me a pass to work for myself, ; so I obtained work by the piece where I could, and paid him out of my earnings what we had agreed on; I maintained myself on the rest, and saved what I could. In this way I was not liable to be flogged and ill-used. He paid seventy, eighty, or ninety dollars a year for me, and I paid him twenty or thirty dollars a year more than that.

When my master came of age, he took all his coloured people to himself. Seeing that I was industrious and persevering, and had obtained plenty of work, he made me pay him almost twice as much as I had paid Mr. Furley. At that time, the English blockaded the Chesapeake, which made it necessary to send merchandize from Norfolk to Elizabeth city by the

Grand Canal, so that it might get to sea by Pamlico Sound and Ocracock Inlet, I took some canal boats on shares; Mr. Grice, who married my other young mistress, was the owner of them. I gave him one-half of all I received for freight: out of the other half, I had to victual and man the boats, and all over that expense was my own profit.

Some time before this, my brother Benjamin returned from the West Indies, where he had been two years with his master's vessel. I was very glad to hear of it, and got leave to go see him. While I was sitting with his wife and him, his wife's master came and asked him to fetch a can of water: he did so, and carried it into the store. While I was waiting for him and wondering at his being so long away, I heard the heavy blows of a hammer: after a little while I was alarmed, and went to see what was going on. I looked into the store, and saw my brother lying on his back on the floor, and Mr. Williams, who had bought him, driving staples over his wrists and ankles; an iron bar was afterwards put across his breast, which was also held down by staples.

I asked what he had been doing, and was told that he had done nothing amiss, but that his master had failed, and he was sold towards paying the debts. He lay in that state all that night; next day he was taken to jail, and I never saw him again. This is the usual treatment under such circumstances. I had to go by my mother's next morning, but I feared to tell her what had happened to my brother: I got a boy to go and tell her.

She was blind and very old, and was living in a little hut, in the woods, after the usual manner of old worn-out slaves: she was unable to go to my brother before he was taken away, and grieved after him greatly.

It was some time after this, that I married a slave belonging to Mr. Enoch Sawyer, who had been so hard a master to me. I left her at home, (that is, at his house,) one Thursday morning, when we had been married about eight months. She was well, and seemed likely to be so: we were nicely getting together our little necessaries. On the Friday, as I was at work as usual with the boats, I heard a noise behind me, on the road which ran by the side of the canal: I turned to look, and saw a gang of slaves coming. When they came up to me, one of them cried out, "Moses, my dear!" I wondered who among them should know me, and found it was my wife. She cried out to me, "I am gone." I was struck with consternation. Mr. Rogerson was with them, on his horse, armed with pistols. I said to him, "for God's sake, have you bought my wife?" He said he had; when I asked him what she had done; he said she had done nothing, but that her master wanted money. He drew out a pistol, and said that if I went near the waggon on which she was, he would shoot me. I asked for leave to shake hands with her, which he refused, but said I might stand at a distance and talk with her. My heart was so full, that I could say very little. I asked leave to give her a dram: he told Mr. Burgess, the man who was with him, to get down and carry it to her. I gave her the little money I had in my pocket, and bid her farewell. I have never seen or heard of her from that day to this. I loved her as I loved my life.

Mr. Grice found that I served him faithfully. He and my young mistress, his wife, advised me as I was getting money fast, to try to buy myself. By their advice, I asked my master what he would take for me. He wanted 800 dollars, and when I said that was too much, he replied, he could get 1000 for me any minute. Mr. Grice afterwards went with me to him: he said to him, that I had already been more profitable to him than any five others of his negroes, and reminded him that we had been playfellows; in this way he got him to consent to take 600 dollars for me. I then went heartily to work, and whenever I paid him for my time, I paid him something also towards my freedom, for which he gave me receipts. When I made him the last payment of the 600 dollars for my freedom, he tore up all the receipts: I told him he ought not to have done so; he replied it did not signify, for as soon as court-day came, he should give me my free papers. On Monday, in court week, I went to him; he was playing at billiards, and would not go with me, but told me to come again the next day: the next day he did the same, and so on daily. I went to his sister, Mrs. Grice, and told her I feared that he did not mean to give them to me; she said she feared so too, and sent for him. He was a very wicked young man; he came, and cursed her, and went out of the house. Mr. Grice was from home; on his return, he went to my master and told him he ought to give me my free papers; that I had paid for myself, and it was court week, so that there was no excuse. He promised he would, instead of which he rode away, and kept away till court was over. Before the next court came, he sold me to Mr. Trewitt for 600 dollars.

The way in which Mr. Trewitt came to buy me, was this. I had left the boats, and had gone with a schooner collecting lumber in Albemarle Sound for the merchants. Coming to Elizabeth City, I found a new store had been opened by Mr. Grice, which Mr. Sutton was keeping: the latter gentleman was glad to see me, and was desirous that I should return to my old employment with the canal boats, as lumber was in great demand at Norfolk. I did so, and sold some cargoes to Mr. Moses Myers of Norfolk. As I was waiting, at the door of his store for settlement, he came up with Mr. Trewitt, whom I did not then know. Mr. Myers said to Mr. Trewitt, "here is a captain doing business for you." Mr. Trewitt then asked me who had chartered the boats, and to whom I belonged. I told him Mr. Sutton had chartered me, and that I had belonged to Mr. James Grandy, but had bought myself. He said he would buy me; on which Mr. Myers told him he could not, as I had already bought myself, and further said, I was one of their old war captains, and had never lost a single thing of the property entrusted to me. Mr. Trewitt said, he would buy me, and would see about it as soon as he got to Elizabeth City. I thought no more about it. On my return voyage, I delivered a cargo at Elizabeth City for Mr. Trewitt. I had been at Mr. Grice's, the owner of the boats, and on my going away from him to meet Mr. Trewitt for settlement, he said he would go with me, as he wanted money. Opposite the Custom House we met Mr. Trewitt, who said, "Well, captain, I have bought you." Mr. Grice said, "Let us have no nonsense; go and settle with him." Angry words passed between them, one saying he had bought me and the other denying that he had, or could, as I had bought myself already. We all went to Mr. Grice's dwelling house; there Mr. Trewitt settled with me about the freight, and then, jumping up, said, "Now I will show you, Mr. Grice, whether I am a liar or not." He fetched the bill of sale; on reading it, Mr. Grice's colour changed, and he sent for Mrs. Grice. When she read it, she began to cry; seeing that, I began to cry too. She sent me to her brother, who was at Mr. Wood's boarding house. He was playing at billiards. I said to him, "Master James, have you sold me?" He said "No." I said, he had; when he turned round and went into another room, crying; I followed him. All the gentlemen followed us, saying, "Captain Grandy, what is the matter?" I told them Master James had sold me again. They asked him why he had done it: he said it was because people had jeered him, by saying I had more sense than he had. They would not suffer him to remain in the boarding house, but turned him out, there and then, with all his trunks and boxes. Mrs. Grice, his sister, sued him in my name for my liberty, but he gained the cause: the court maintained that I, and all I could do, belonged to him, and that he had a right to do as he pleased with me and all my earnings, as his own property, until he had taken me to the Court House, and given me my free papers, and until, besides that, I had been a year and a day in the Northern States to gain my residence.

So I was forced to go to Mr. Trewitt. He agreed that, if I would pay him the same wages as I paid my late master, and the 600 dollars he gave for me, he would give me my free papers. He bought two canal boats; and taking me out of Mr. Grice's employment, set me to work them on the same terms as I did for my former master. I was two years and a half in earning the 600 dollars to pay for myself the second time. Just when I had completed the payment, he failed. Oh Christmas eve he gave me a letter to take to Mr. Mews, at Newbegun Creek. I was rather unwilling to take it, wishing to go to my wife; I told him, too, I was going to his office to settle with him. He offered to give me two dollars to take the letter, and said he would settle when I came back: then Mr. Shaw came from another room, and said his vessel was ready loaded, but he had nobody he could trust with his goods; he offered me five dollars to take the vessel down, and deliver the goods to Mr. Knox, who also was at Newbegun Creek. The wind was fair, and the hands on board, so I agreed: it being Christmas eve, I was glad of something to carry to my wife. I ran the vessel down to the mouth of the

Creek, and anchored: when the moon rose, I went up the river. I reached the wharf, and commenced taking out the goods that night, and delivered them all safely to Mr. Knox next morning. I then took the letter to Mr. Mews, who read it, and looking up at me said, "Well, you belong to me." I thought he was joking, and said, "How? What way?" He said, "Don't you recollect when Trewitt chartered Wilson Sawyer's brig to the West Indies?" I said, I did. He told me Trewitt then came to him to borrow 600 dollars, which he would not lend except he had a mortgage on me: Trewitt was to take it up at a certain time, but never did. I asked him, whether he really took the mortgage on me? He replied that "he certainly thought Trewitt would have taken up the mortgage, but he had failed, and was not worth a cent, and he, Mews, must have his money." I asked him whether he had not helped me and my young mistress in the Court House, when Master James fooled me before? He said he did help me all he could, and that he should not have taken a mortgage on me, but that he thought Trewitt would take it up. Trewitt must have received some of the last payments from me, after he had given the mortgage, and knew he should fail; for the mortgage was given two months before this time.

My head seemed to turn round and round; I was quite out of my senses; I went away towards the woods; Mr. Mews sent his waiter after me, to persuade me to go back: at first I refused, but afterwards went. He told me he would give me another chance to buy myself, and I certainly should have my freedom this time. He said Mr. Enoch Sawyer wanted to buy me to be his overseer in the Swamp. I replied, I would never try again to buy myself, and that they had already got 1200 dollars from me. My wife, (this was my second (It will be observed that the narrator married a second wife, without having heard of the decease of the first. To explain this fact, it is necessary to state, that the frequent occurrence of cases where husbands and wives, members of Christian societies, were finally separated by sale, led the ministers, some years ago, to deliberate on the subject: they decided that such a separation might be considered as the death of the parties to each other, and they therefore agreed to consider subsequent marriages not immoral. The practice is general. It is scarcely necessary to remark that a more unequivocal and impressive proof of the heinous nature of the system could hardly exist. It breaks up the fondest connexions, it tears up the holiest attachments, and induces the ministers of religion, as much as in them lies, to garble the divine law to suit its own infernal exigencies.) wife) belonged to Mr. Sawyer: he told me that her master would not allow me to go to see her, if I would not consent to what he now preposed: for any coloured person going on the grounds of a white man after being warned of, is liable to be flogged or even shot. I thus found myself forced to go, although no coloured man wishes to live at the house where his wife lives, for he has to endure the continual misery of seeing her flogged and abused, without daring to say a word in her defence.

In the service of Mr. Sawyer, I got into a fair way of buying myself again; for I undertook the lightering of the shingles or boards out of the Dismal Swamp, and hired hands to assist me. But my master had become security for his two sons-in-law at Norfolk, who failed; in consequence of which, he sold eighteen coloured people, his share of the Swamp, and two plantations. I was one of the slaves he kept, and after that had to work in the corn-field the same as the rest. The overseer was a bad one, his name was Brooks. The horn was blown at sunrise; the coloured people had then to march before the overseer to the field, He on horseback. We had to work, even in long, summer days, till twelve o'clock, before we tasted a morsel; men, women, and children all being served alike. At noon the cart appeared with our breakfast. It was in large trays, and was set on the ground. There was bread, of which a piece was cut off for each person; then there was small hominy boiled, (that is, Indian corn, ground in the hand-mill) and besides this, two herrings for each of the men and women, and one for each of the children. Our drink was the water in the ditches, whatever might be its state; if the ditches were dry, water was brought to us by boys. The salt fish made us always thirsty, but no other drink than water was ever allowed. However thirsty a slave may be, he is not allowed to leave his employment for a moment to get water; he can only have it when the hands in working have reached the ditch at the end of the rows. The overseer stood with his watch in his hand, to give us just an hour; when he said "rise," we had to rise and go to work again. The women who had children laid them down by the hedge-row, and gave them straws and other trifles to play with: here they were in danger from snakes. I have seen a large snake found coiled round the neck and face of a child, when its mother went to suckle it at dinner time. The hands work in a line, by the side of each other; the overseer puts the swiftest hands in the fore row, and all must keep up with them. One black man is kept on purpose to whip the others in the field; if he does not flog with sufficient severity, he is flogged himself: he whips severely, to keep the whip from his own back. If a man has a wife in the same field with himself; he chooses a row by the side of hers, that with extreme labour he may, if possible, help her. But he will not be in the same field if he can help it; for with his hardest labour, he often cannot save her from being flogged, and he is obliged to stand by and see it; he is always liable to see her taken home at night, stripped naked, and whipped before all the men. On the estate I am speaking of, those women who had sucking children suffered much from their breasts becoming full of milk, the infants being left at home; they therefore could not keep up with the other hands: I seen the overseer beat them with raw hide, so that blood and milk flew mingled from their breasts. A woman who gives offence in the field, and is large in the family way, is compelled to lie down over a hole made to receive her, and is then flogged with the whip, or beaten with a paddle, which has holes in it; at every hole comes a blister. One of my sisters was so severely punished in this way, that labour was brought on, and the child was born in the field. This very overseer, Mr. Brooks, killed in this manner a girl named Mary: her father and mother were in the field at the time. He also killed a boy about twelve years old. He had no punishment, or even trial, for either.

There was no dinner till dark, when he gave the order to knock off and go home. The meal then was the same as in the morning) except that we had meat twice a-week.

On very few estates are the coloured people provided with any bedding; the best masters give only a blanket; this master gave none. A board, which the slave might pick up anywhere on the estate, was all he had to lie on. If he wished to procure bedding, he could only do so by working at nights. For warmth, therefore, the negroes generally sleep near a large fire, whether in the kitchen, or in their log, huts; their legs are often in this way blistered and greatly swelled, and sometimes badly burnt: they suffer severely from this cause.

When the water-mill did not supply meal enough, we had to grind with the hand-mill. The night was employed in this work, without any thing being taken from the labour of the day. We had to take turn at it, women as well as men; enough was to be ground to serve for the following day.

I was eight months in the field. My master, Mr. Sawyer, agreed to allow me eight dollars a month, while so employed, towards buying myself: it will be seen he did not give me even that. When I first went to work in the corn field, I had paid him 230 dollars towards this third buying of my freedom. I told him one night, I could not stand his field work any longer; he asked, why; I said I was almost starved to death, and had long been unaccustomed to this severe labour. He wanted to know why I could not stand it as well as the rest. I told him, he knew well I had not been used to it for a long time; that his overseer was the worst that had ever been on the plantation, and that I could not stand it. He said he would direct Mr. Brooks to give each of us a pint of meal or corn every evening, which we might bake, and which would serve us next morning, till our breakfast came at noon. The black people were much rejoiced that I got this additional allowance for them. But I was not satisfied; I wanted liberty.

One Sunday morning, as Master was sitting in his porch, I went to him and offered to give him the 230 dollars I had already paid him, if, beside them, he would take for my freedom the 600 dollars he had given for me. He drove me away, saying, I had no way to get the money. I sat down for a time, and went to him again: I repeated my offer to procure the 600 dollars, and he again said, I could not. He called his wife out of the room to the porch, and said to her, "Don't you think Moses has taken to getting drunk?" She asked me if it was so; I denied it, when she inquired what was the matter. Master replied, "Don't you think he wants me to sell him?" She said, "Moses, we would not take any money for you. Captain Cormack put a thousand dollars for you on the supper table last Friday night, and Mr. Sawyer would not touch it: he wants you to be overseer in the Dismal Swamp." I replied, "Captain Cormack never said anything to me about buying me: I would cut my throat from ear to ear rather than go to him. I know what made him say so; he is courting Miss Patsey, and he did it to make himself look big". Mistress laughed and turned away, and slammed to the door: Master shook himself with laughing, and put the paper he was reading before his face, knowing that I spoke the truth. Captain Cormack was an old man who went on crutches: Miss Patsey was the finest of master's daughters. Master drove me away from him again.

On Monday morning, Mr. Brooks, the overseer, blew the horn as usual for all to go to the field. I refused to go. I went to master and told him that if he would give me a paper, I would go and fetch the 600 dollars; he then gave me a paper, stating that he was willing to take that sum for my freedom; so I hired an old horse and started for Norfolk; fifty miles off.

When I reached Deep Creek, I went to the house of Captain Edward Minner. He was very glad to see me, for in former days I had done much business for him: he said how sorry he had been to hear that I was at field-work. He inquired where I was going. I said to Norfolk, to get some of the merchants to let me have money to buy myself. He replied, "What did I always say to you? Was it not, that I would let you have the money at any time, if you would only tell me when you could be sold?" He called Mrs. Minner into the room, and told her I could be sold for my freedom: she was rejoiced to hear it. He said, "Put up your horse at Mr. Western's Tavern, for you need go no farther; I have plenty of old rusty dollars, and no man shall put his hand on your collar again to say you are a slave. Come and stay with me to-night, and in the morning I will get Mr. Garrett's horse, and go with you."

Next morning we set off, and found master at Major Farrance's, at the cross canal, where I knew he was to be that day, to sell his share of the canal. When I saw him he told me to go forward home, for he would not sell me. I felt sick and sadly disappointed. Captain Minner stepped up to him and shewed him the paper he had given me, saying, "Mr. Sawyer, is not this your handwriting?" He replied, "Mistress said, the last word when I came away, I was not to sell him, but send him home again." Captain Minner said, "Mind, gentlemen, I do not want him for a slave; I want to buy him for freedom. He will repay me the money, and I shall not charge him a cent of interest for it. I would not have a coloured person to drag me down to hell, for all the money in the world." A gentleman who was by said it was a shame I should be so treated; I had bought myself so often that Mr. Sawyer ought to let me go. The very worst man as an overseer over the persons employed in digging the canal, Mr. Wiley M'Pherson, was there: he was never known to speak in favour of a coloured person; even he said that Mr. Sawyer ought to let me go, as I had been sold so often. At length Mr. Sawyer consented I should go for 650 dollars and would take no less. I wished Captain Minner to give the extra 50 dollars, and not to stand about it. I believe it was what M'Pherson said that induced my master to let me go: for he was well known for his great severity to coloured people, so that after even he had said so, master could not stand out. The Lord must have opened M'Pherson's heart to say it.

I have said this M'Pherson was an overseer where slaves were employed in cutting canals. The labour there is very severe. The ground is often very boggy: the negroes are up to the middle or much deeper in mud and water, cutting away roots and baling out mud: if they can keep their heads above water, they work on. They lodge in huts, or as they are called camps, made of shingles or boards. They lie down in the mud which has adhered to them, making a great fire to dry themselves, and keep off the cold. No bedding whatever is allowed them; it is only by work done over his task, that any of them can get a blanket. They are paid nothing except for this overwork. Their masters come once a month to receive the money for their labour: then perhaps some few very good masters will give them two dollars each, some others one dollar, some a pound of tobacco, and some nothing at all. The food is more abundant than that of field slaves; indeed it is the best allowance in America: it consists of a peck of meal, and six pounds of pork per week; the pork is commonly not good, it is damaged, and is bought as cheap as possible at auctions.

M'Pherson gave the same task to each slave; of course the weak ones often failed to do it. I have often seen him tie up persons and flog them in the morning, only because they were unable to get the previous day's task done: after they were flogged, pork or beef brine was put on their bleeding backs, to increase the pain; he sitting by resting himself, and seeing it done. After being thus flogged and pickled, the sufferers often remained tied up all day, the feet just touching the ground, the legs tied, and pieces of wood put between the legs. All the motion allowed was a slight turn of the neck. Thus exposed and helpless, the yellow flies and musquitoes in great numbers would settle on the bleeding and smarting back, and put the sufferer to extreme torture. This continued all day, for they were not taken down till night. In flogging, he would sometimes tie the slave's shirt over his head, that he might not flinch when the blow was coming: sometimes he would increase his misery, by blustering and calling out that he was coming to flog again, which he did or did not, as happened. I have seen him flog slaves with his own hands, till their entrails were visible; and I have seen the sufferers dead when they were taken down. He never was called to account in any way for it.

It is not uncommon for flies to blow the sores made by flogging. In that case, we get a strong weed growing in those parts, called the Oak of Jerusalem; we boil it at night, and wash the sores with the liquor, which is extremely bitter: on this, the creepers or maggots come out. To relieve them in some degree after severe flogging, their fellow-slaves rub their backs with part of their little allowance of fat meat.

For fear the slaves should run away, while unable to work from flogging, He kept them chained till they could work again. This man had from 500 to 700 men under his control. When out of other employment, I sometimes worked under him, and saw his doings. I believe it was the word of this man which gained my freedom. He is dead, but there are yet others like him on public works.

When the great kindness of Captain Minner had set me clear of Mr. Enoch Sawyer, I went to my old occupation of working the canal boats. These I took on shares as before. After a time, I was disabled for a year from following this employment by a severe attack of rheumatism, caught by frequent exposure to severe weather. I was anxious however to be earning something towards the repayment of Captain Minner, lest any accident unforeseen by him or me, should even yet deprive me of the liberty for which I so longed, and for which I had suffered so much. I therefore had myself carried in a lighter up a cross canal in the Dismal Swamp, and to the other side of Drummond's Lake. I was left on the shore and there I built myself a little hut, and had provisions brought to me as opportunity served. Here, among, snakes, bears, and panthers, whenever my strength was sufficient, I cut down a juniper tree, and converted it into cooper's timber. The camp, like those commonly set up for negroes, was entirely open on one side; on that side a fire is lighted at night, and the person sleeping puts his feet towards it. One night I was awoke by some large animal smelling my face, and snuffing strongly; I felt its cold muzzle. I suddenly thrust out my arms, and shouted with all my might; it was frightened and made off. I do not know whether it was a bear or a panther, but it seemed as tall as a large calf. I slept of course no more that night. I put my trust in the Lord, and continued on the spot; I was never attacked again.

I recovered, and went to the canal boats again. By the end of three years from the time he laid down the money, I entirely repaid my very kind and excellent friend. During this time he made no claim whatever on my services; I was altogether on the footing of a free man, as far as a coloured man can there be free.

When, at length, I had repaid Captain Minner, and had got my free papers, so that my freedom was quite secure, my feelings were greatly excited. I felt to myself so light, that I almost thought I could fly, and in my sleep I was always dreaming of flying over woods and rivers. My gait was so altered by my gladness, that people often stopped me, saying, "Grandy, what is the matter?" I excused myself as well as I could; but many perceived the reason, and said, "Oh ! he is so pleased with having got his freedom." Slavery will teach any man to be glad when he gets freedom.

My good master, Captain Minner, sent me to Providence, in Rhode Island, to stay a year and a day in order to gain my residence. But I stayed only two months. Mr. Howard's vessel came there laden with corn. I longed much to see my master and mistress for the kindness they had done me, and so went home in the schooner. On my arrival, I did not stop at my own house, except to ask my wife at the door how she and the children were in health, but went up the town to see Captain and Mrs. Minner. They were very glad to see me, and consulted with me about my way of getting a living. I wished to go on board the New York and Philadelphia Packets, but feared I should be troubled for my freedom. Captain Minner thought I might venture, and I therefore engaged myself. I continued in that employment till his death, which happened about a year after my return from Providence. Then I returned to Boston; for, while he lived, I knew I could rely on his protection; but when I lost my friend, I thought it best to go wholly to the Northern States.

At Boston I went to work at sawing wood, sawing with the whip-saw, labouring in the coal yards, loading and unloading vessels, &c. After labouring in this way for a few months, I went a voyage to St. John's in Porto Rico, with Captain Cobb, in the schooner, *New Packet*. On the return voyage, the vessel got ashore on Cape Cod: we left her, after doing in vain what we could to right her; she was afterwards recovered. I went several other voyages, and particularly two to the Mediterranean. The last was to the East Indies, in the ship *James Murray*, Captain Woodbury; owner, Mr. Gray. My entire savings up to the period of my return from this voyage amounted to 300 dollars; I sent it to Virginia, and bought my wife. She came to me at Boston. I dared not go myself to fetch her, lest I should be again deprived of my liberty, as often happens to free coloured people.

At the time called the time of the Insurrection, about eight years ago, when the whites said the coloured people were going to rise, and shot, hanged, and otherwise destroyed many of them, Mrs. Minner thought she saw me in the street, and fainted there. The soldiers were seizing all the blacks they could find, and she knew if I were there, I should be sure to suffer with the rest. She was mistaken; I was not there.

My son's master at Norfolk sent a letter to me at Boston to say, that if I could raise 450 dollars, I might have his freedom; he was then fifteen years old. I had again saved 300 dollars. I knew the master was a drinking man, and I was therefore very anxious to get my son out of his hands. I went to Norfolk running the risk of my liberty, and took my 300 dollars with me, to make the best bargain I could. Many gentlemen, my friends, in Boston, advised me not to go myself: but I was anxious to get my boy's freedom, and I knew that nobody in Virginia had any cause of complaint against me; so, notwithstanding their advice, I determined to go.

When the vessel arrived there, they said it was against the law for me to go ashore. The mayor of the city said, I had been among the cursed Yankees too long. He asked me whether I did not know, that it was unlawful for me to land; to which I replied, that I did not know it, for I could neither read nor write. The merchants for whom I had formerly done business came on board, and said they cared for neither the mare (mayor) nor the horse, and insisted that I should go ashore. I told the mayor the business on which I came, and he gave me leave to stay nine days, telling me that if I were not gone in that time, he would sell me for the good of the State.

I offered my boy's master the 300 dollars: he counted the money, but put it back to me, refusing to take less than 450 dollars. I went on board, to return to Boston. We met with head winds, and put back three times to Norfolk, anchoring each time Just opposite the jail. The nine days had expired, and I feared the mayor would find me on board and sell me. I could see the jail full of coloured people, and even the whipping post, at which they were constantly enduring the lash. While we were lying there by the jail, two vessels came from Eastern

Shore, Virginia, laden with cattle and coloured people. The cattle were lowing for their calves, and the men and women were crying for their husbands, wives, or children. The cries and groans were terrible, notwithstanding there was a whipper on board each vessel, trying to compel the poor creatures to keep silence. These vessels lay close to ours.

I had been a long time away from such scenes; the sight affected me very much, and added greatly to my fears.

One day, I saw a boat coming from the shore with white men in it. I thought they were officers coming to take me; and such was my horror of slavery, that I twice ran to the ship's waist, to jump overboard into the strong ebb-tide then running, to drown myself: but a strong impression on my mind restrained me each time.

Once more we got under way for New York; but meeting again with head winds, we ran into Maurice's River, in Delaware Bay. New Jersey, in which that place lies, is not a slave state. So I said to the captain, "Let me have a boat, and set me on the free land once-more, then I will travel home overland; for I will not run the risk of going back to Virginia any more." The captain said there was no danger, but I exclaimed, "No! no! captain, I will not try it; put my feet on free land once again, and I shall be safe." When I once more touched the free land, the burthen of my mind was removed: if two ton weight had been taken of me, the relief would not have seemed so great.

From Maurice's Creek I traveled to Philadelphia, and at that place had a letter written to my wife at Boston, thanking God that I was on free land again. On arriving at Boston, I borrowed 160 dollars of a friend, and going to New York I obtained the help of Mr. John Williams to send the 450 dollars to Norfolk: thus, at length, I bought my son's freedom. I met him at New York, and brought him on to Boston.

Six others of my children, three boys and three girls, were sold to New Orleans. Two of these daughters have bought their own freedom. The eldest of them, Catherine, was sold three times after she was taken away from Virginia: the first time was by auction. Her last master but one was a Frenchman: she worked in his sugar-cane and cotton fields. Another Frenchman inquired for a girl on whom he could depend, to wait on his wife, who was in a consumption. Her master offered him my daughter; they went into the field to see her, and the bargain was struck. Her new master gave her up to his sick wife, on whom she waited till her death. As she had waited exceedingly well on his wife, her master offered her a chance of buying her freedom. She objected to his terms as too high; for he required her to pay him four dollars a week out of her earnings, and 1200 dollars for her freedom. He said he could get more for her, and told her she might get plenty of washing at a dollar a dozen; at last she agreed. She lived near the river side, and obtained plenty of work. So anxious was she to obtain her freedom, that she worked nearly all her time, days and nights, and Sundays. She found, however, she gained nothing by working on Sundays, and therefore left it off. She paid her master punctually her weekly hire and also something towards her freedom, for which he gave her receipts. A good stewardess was wanted for a steam boat on the Mississippi; she was hired for the place at thirty dollars a-month, which is the usual salary: she also had liberty to sell apples and oranges on board; and commonly, the passengers give from twenty-five cents to a dollar, to a stewardess who attends them Well. Her entire incoming, wages and all, amounted to about sixty dollars a-month. She remained at this employment till she had paid the entire sum of 1200 dollars for her freedom.

As soon as she obtained her free papers, she left the steam-boat, thinking she could find her sister Charlotte. Her two first trials were unsuccessful: but On the third attempt she found her at work in the cane-field. She shewed her sister's master her own free papers, and told him how she had bought herself: he said, that if her sister would pay him as much as she paid her master, she might go too. They agreed, and he gave her a pass. The two sisters went on board a steam-boat, and worked together for the wages of one, till they had saved the entire 1200 dollars for the freedom of the second sister. The husband of Charlotte was dead: her children were left behind in the cotton and cane-fields; their master refuses to take less than 2400 dollars for them: their names and ages are as follows: Zeno, about fifteen; Antoinette, about thirteen; Joseph, about eleven; and Josephine about ten years old.

Of my other children, I only know that one, a girl named Betsy, is a little way from Norfolk in Virginia. Her master, Mr. William Dixon, is willing to sell her for 500 dollars.

I do not know where any of my other four children are, nor whether they be dead or alive. It will be very difficult to find them out; for the names of slaves are commonly changed with every change of master: they usually bear the name of the master to whom they belong at the time. They have no family name of their own by which they can be traced. Owing to this circumstance, and their ignorance of reading and writing, to which they are compelled by law, all trace between parents and their children who are separated from them in childhood, is lost in a few years. When, therefore, a child is sold away from its mother, she feels that she is parting from it for ever: there is little likelihood of her ever knowing what of good or evil befals it. The way of finding out a friend or relative, who has been sold away for any length of time, or to any great distance, is to trace him, if possible, to one master after another; or if that cannot be done, to inquire about the neighbourhood where he is supposed to be, until some one is found who can tell that such a person belonged to such or such a master: and the person supposed to be the one sought for, may perhaps remember the names of the persons to whom his father and mother belonged. There is little to be learnt from his appearance, for so many years may have passed away, that he may have grown out of the memory of his parents, or his nearest relations. There are thus no lasting family ties to bind relations together, not even the nearest, and this aggravates their distress when they are sold from each other. I have little hope of finding my four children again.

I have lived at Boston ever since I bought my freedom, except during the last year, which I have spent at Portland, in the state of Maine.

I have yet said nothing of my father. He was often sold through the failure of his successive owners. When I was a little boy, he was sold away from us to a distance: he was then so far off, that he could not come to see us oftener than once a year. After that, he was sold to go still further away, and then he could not come at all. I do not know what has become of him.

When my mother became old, she was sent to live in a little lonely log-hut in the woods. Aged and worn out slaves, whether men or women, are commonly so treated. No care is taken of them, except, perhaps, that a little ground is cleared about the hut, on which the old slave, if able, may raise a little corn. As far as the owner is concerned, they live or die as it happens; is is just the same thing as turning out an old horse. Their children or other near relations, if living in the neighbourhood, take it by turns to go at night, with a supply saved out of their own scanty allowance of food, as well as to cut wood and fetch water for them: this is done entirely through the good feelings of the slaves, and not through the masters' taking care that it is done. On these night-visits, the aged inmate of the hut is often found crying, on account of sufferings from disease or extreme weakness, or from want of food and water in the course of the day: many a time, when I have drawn near to my mother's hut, I have heard her grieving and crying on these accounts: she was old and blind too, and so unable to help herself. She was not treated worse than others: it is the general practice. Some few good masters do not treat their old slaves so: they employ them in doing light jobs about the house and garden.

My eldest sister is in Elizabeth City. She has five children, who, of course, are slaves. Her master is willing to sell her for 100 dollars: she is growing old. One of her children, a young man, cannot be bought under 900 dollars.

My sister Tamar, who belonged to the same master with myself, had children very fast. Her husband had hard owners, and lived at a distance. When a woman who has many children belongs to an owner who is under age, as ours was, it is customary to put her and the children out yearly to the person who will maintain them for the least money, the person taking them having the benefit of whatever work the woman can do. But my sister was put to herself in the woods. She had a bit of ground cleared, and was left to hire herself out to labour. On the ground she raised corn and flax; and obtained a peck of corn, some herrings, or a piece of meat for a day's work among the neighbouring owners. In this way she brought up her children. Her husband could help her but little. As soon as each of the children became big enough, it was sold away from her.

After parting thus with five, she was sold along with the sixth, (about a year and a half old,) to the speculators; these are persons who buy slaves in Carolina and Virginia, to sell them in Georgia and New Orleans. After travelling with them more than 100 miles, she made her escape, but could not obtain her child to take it with her. On her journey homeward, she traveled by night, and hid herself in thick woods by day. She was in great danger on the road, but in three weeks reached the woods near us. There she had to keep herself concealed; I, my mother, and her husband knew where she was: she lived in a den she made for herself. She sometimes ventured down to my mother's hut, where she was hid in a hollow under the floor. Her husband lived twenty-five miles off: he would sometimes set off after his day's work was done, spend part of the night with her, and get back to work before next sunrise: sometimes he would spend Sunday with her. We all supplied her with such provisions as we could save. It was necessary to be very careful in visiting her; we tied pieces of wood or bundles of rags to our feet that no track might be made.

In the wood she had three children born; one of them died. She had not recovered from the birth of the youngest, when she was discovered and taken to the house of her old master. She was afterwards sold to Culpepper, who used her very cruelly. He was beating her dreadfully, and the blood was streaming from her head and back, one day when I happened to go to his house. I was greatly grieved, and asked his leave to find a person to buy her: instead of answering me, he struck at me with an axe, and I was obliged to get away as fast as I could. Soon after, he failed, and she was offered for sale in Norfolk; there Mr. Johnson bought her and her two children, out of friendship for me: he treated her exceedingly well, and she served him faithfully: but it was not long before she was claimed by a person, to whom Culpepper had mortgaged her before he sold her to Johnson. This person sold her to Long, of Elizabeth City, where again she was very badly treated. After a time, Long sold her to go to Georgia: she was very in at the time, and was taken away in a cart. I hear from her sometimes, and am very anxious to purchase her freedom, if ever I should be able. Two of her children are now in North Carolina, and are longing to obtain their freedom.

I know nothing of the others, nor am I likely ever to hear of them again.

The treatment of slaves is mildest near the borders, where the free and slave states join: it becomes more severe, the further we go from the free states. It is more severe in the west and south than where I lived. The sale of slaves most frequently takes place from the milder to the severer parts: in that directtion, there is great traffic in slaves, which is carried on by the speculators. On the frontier between the slave and free states there is a guard; no coloured person can go over a ferry without a pass. By these regulations, and the great numbers of patrols, escape is made very difficult.

Formerly slaves were allowed to have religious meetings of their own; but after the insurrection which I spoke of before, they were forbidden to meet even for worship. Often they are flogged, if they are found singing or praying at home. They may go to the places of worship used by the whites; but they like their own meetings better. My wife's brother Isaac was a coloured preacher. A number of slaves went privately into the wood to hold meetings; when they were found out, they were flogged, and each was forced to tell who else was there. Three were shot, two of whom were killed, and the other was badly wounded. For preaching to them, Isaac was flogged, and his back pickled; when he was nearly well, he was flogged and pickled again, and so on for some months; then his back was suffered to get well, and he was sold. A little while before this, his wife was sold away with an infant at her breast; and of his six children, four had been sold away by one at a time. On the way with his buyers he dropped down dead; his heart was broken.

Having thus narrated what has happened to myself, my relatives, and near friends, I will add a few matters about slaves and coloured persons in general.

Slaves are under fear in every word they speak. If in their master's kitchen they let slip an expression of discontent, or a wish for freedom, it is often reported to the master or mistress by the children of the family, who may be playing about: severe flogging is often the consequence.

I have already said that it is forbidden by law to teach coloured persons to read or write. A few well disposed white young persons, of the families to which the slaves belonged, have ventured to teach them, but they dare not let it be known they have done so.

The proprietors get new land cleared in this way. They first "dead" a piece of ground in the woods adjoining the plantation. By "deading" is meant killing the trees, by cutting a nick all round each, quite through the bark. Out of this ground each coloured person has a piece as large as he can tend after his other work is done: the women have pieces in like manner. The slave works at night, cutting down the timber and clearing the ground; after it is cleared, he has it for his own use for two or three years, as may be agreed on. As these new clearings lie between the woods and the old cultivated land, the squirrels and racoons first come at the crops on them, and thus those on the planters' land are saved from much waste. When the negro has had the land for the specified time, and it has become fit for the plough, the master takes it, and he is removed to another new piece. It is no uncommon thing for the land to be taken from him before the time is out, if it has sooner become fit for the plough. When the crop is gathered, the master comes to see how much there is of it; he then gives the negro an order to sell that quantity; without that order, no storekeeper dare buy it. The slave lays out the money in something tidy, to go to meeting in, and something to take to his wife.

The evidence of a black man, or of ever so many black men, stands for nothing against that of one white; in consequence of this, the free negroes are liable to great cruelties. They have had their dwellings entered, their bedding and furniture destroyed, themselves, their wives, and children beaten; some have even been taken, with their wives, into the woods, and tied up, flogged, and left there. There is nothing which a white man may not do against a black one, if he only takes care that no other white man can give evidence against him.

A law has lately been passed in New Orleans, prohibiting any free coloured person from going there.

The coasting packets of the ports on the Atlantic, commonly have coloured cooks. When a vessel goes from New York or Boston to a port in the slave-holding estates, the black cook is usually put in jail till the vessel sails again.

No coloured person can travel without a pass. If he cannot show it, he may be flogged by any body; in such a case, he often is seized and flogged by the patrols. all through the slave states there are patrols; they are so numerous that they cannot easily be escaped.

The only time when a man can visit his wife, when they are on different estates, is Saturday evening and Sunday. If they be very near to each other, he may sometimes see her on Wednesday evening. He must always return to his work by sunrise; if he fail to do so, he is flogged. When he has got together all the little things he can for his wife and children, and has walked many miles to see them, he may find that they have all been sold away, some in one direction, and some in another.

He gives up all hope of seeing them again, but he dare not utter a word of complaint.

It often happens that when a slave wishes to visit his wife on another plantation, his own master is busy or from home, and therefore he cannot get a pass. He ventures without it. If there be any little spite against his wife, or himself, he maybe asked for it when he arrives; and not having it, he may be beaten with thirty-nine stripes, and sent away. On his return he may be seized by the patrol, and flogged again for the same reason, and he will not wonder if he is again seized and beaten for the third time.

If a negro has given offence to the patrol, even by so innocent a matter as dressing tidily to go to a place of worship, he will be seized by one of them, and another will tear up his pass: while one is flogging him, the others will look another way; so when he or his master make complaint of his having been beaten without cause, and he points out the person who did it, the others will swear they saw no one beat him. His oath, being that of a black man, would stand for nothing, but he may not even be sworn; and in such a case his tormentors are safe, for they were the only whites present.

In all the slave states there are men who make a trade of whipping negroes: they ride about inquiring for jobs of persons who keep no overseer; if there is a negro to be whipped, whether man or woman, this man is employed when he calls, and does it immediately; his fee is half a dollar. Widows and other females having negroes, get them whipped in this way. Many mistresses will insist on the slave who has been flogged, begging pardon for her fault on her knees, and thanking her for the correction.

A white man who lived near me in Camden county, Thomas Evidge, followed this business. He was also sworn-whipper at the Court House. A law was passed that any white man detected in stealing should be whipped. Mr. Dozier frequently missed hogs, and flogged many of his negroes on suspicion of stealing them: when he could not in his suspicions fix on any one in particular, he flogged them all round, saying that he was sure of having punished the right one. Being one day shooting in his woods, he heard the report of another gun, and shortly after met David Evidge, the nephew of the whipper, with one of his hogs on his back which had just been shot: David was sent to prison, convicted of the theft, and sentenced to be flogged. His uncle, who vapoured about greatly in flogging slaves, and taunted them with unfeeling speeches while he did it, could not bear the thought of flogging his nephew, and hired a man to do it. The person pitched on, chanced to be a sailor; he laid it well on the thief: pleased enough were the coloured people to see a white back for the first time subjected to the lash.

Another man of the same business, George Wilkins, did no greater credit to the trade. Mr. Carnie, on Western Branch, Virginia, often missed corn from his barn. Wilkins, the whipper, was very officious in pointing out this slave and that, as very likely to be the thief: with nothing against them but his insinuations, some were severely punished, being flogged by this very Wilkins; and others, at his instigation, were sold away. One night Mr. Carnie, unknown to his coloured people, set a steel trap in the barn. Some of the negroes, passing the barn before morning, saw Wilkins standing there, but were not aware he was caught. They called the master, that he might seize the thief before he could escape: he came and teased Wilkins during the night; in the morning he exposed him to the view of the neighbours, and then set him at liberty without further punishment.

The very severe punishments to which slaves are subjected for trifling offences or none at all, their continued liability to all kinds of in usage without a chance of redress, and the agonizing feelings they endure at being separated from the dearest connexions, drive many of them to desperation, and they abscond. They hide themselves in the woods, where they remain for months, and in some cases for years. When caught, they are flogged with extreme severity, their backs are pickled and the flogging repeated as before described. After months of this torture the back is allowed to heal, and the slave is sold away. Especially is this done when the slave has attempted to reach a free state.

In violent thunder-storms, when the whites have got between feather beds to be safe from the lightning, I have often seen negroes, the aged as well as others, go out, and lifting up their hands, thank God that judgment was coming at last. So cruelly are many of them used, that judgment, they think, would be a happy release from their horrible slavery.

The proprietors, though they live in luxury, generally die in debt: their negroes are so hardly treated, that no profit is made by their labour. Many of them are great gamblers. At the death of a proprietor, it commonly happens that his coloured people are sold towards paying his debts. So it must and will be with the masters, while slavery continues: when freedom is established, I believe they will begin to prosper greatly.

Before I close this narrative, I ought to express my grateful thanks to the many friends in the Northern States, who have encouraged and assisted me: I shall never forget to speak of their kindness, and to pray for their prosperity. I am delighted to say, that not only to myself, but to very many other coloured 66 persons, they have lent a benevolent helping hand. Last year, gentlemen whom I know bought no less than ten families from slavery, and this year they are pursuing the same good work. But for these numerous and heavy claims on their means and their kindness, I should have had no need to appeal to the generosity of the British public; they would gladly have helped me to redeem all my children and relations.

When I first went to the Northern States, which is about ten years ago, although I was free as to the law, I was made to feel severely the difference between persons of different colours. No black man was admitted to the same seats in churches with the whites, nor to the inside of public conveyances, nor into street coaches or cabs: we had to be content with the decks of steam-boats in all weathers, night and day, -- not even our wives or children being allowed to go below, however it might rain, or snow, or freeze; in various other ways, we were treated as though we were of a race of men below the whites. But the abolitionists boldly stood up for us, and through them things are much changed for the better.

Now, we may sit in any part of many places of worship, and are even asked into the pews of respectable white families; many public conveyances now make no distinction between white and black. We begin to feel that we are really on the same footing as our fellow citizens. They see we can and do conduct ourselves with propriety, and they are now admitting us in many cases to the same standing with themselves.

During the struggles which have procured for us this justice from our fellow-citizens, we have been in the habit of looking in public places for some well-known abolitionists, and if none that we knew were there, we addressed any person dressed as a Quaker; these classes always took our part against ill usage, and we have to thank them for many a contest in our behalf.

We were greatly delighted by the zealous efforts and powerful eloquence in our cause of Mr. George Thompson, who came from our English friends to aid our suffering brethren. He was hated and mobbed by bad men amongst the whites; they put his life in great danger, and threatened destruction to all who sheltered him. We prayed for him, and did all we could to defend him. The Lord preserved him, and thankful were we when he escaped from our country with his life. At that time, and ever since, we have had a host of American friends, who have laboured for the cause night and day; they have nobly stood up for the rights and honour of the coloured man; but they did so at first in the midst of scorn and danger. Now, thank God, the case is very different Mr. William Lloyd Garrison, who was hunted for his life by a mob in the streets of Boston has lately been chairman of a large meeting in favour of abolition, held in Fanueil Hall, the celebrated public hall of Boston, called "the Cradle of Liberty."

I am glad to say also, that numbers of my coloured brethren now escape from slavery; some by purchasing their freedom, others by quitting, through many dangers and hardships, the land of bondage. The latter suffer many privations in their attempts to reach the free states. They hide themselves during the day in the woods and swamps; at night they travel, crossing rivers by swimming, or by boats they may chance to meet with, and passing over hills and meadows which they do not know; in these dangerous journeys they are guided by the north-star, for they only know that the land of freedom is in the north. They subsist on such wild fruit as they can gather, and as they are often very long on their way, they reach the free states almost like skeletons. On their arrival, they have no friends but such as pity those who have been in bondage, the number of which, I am happy to say, is increasing; but if they can meet with a man in a broadbrimmed hat and Quaker coat, they speak to him without fear-relying on him as a friend. At each place the escaped slave inquires for an abolitionist or a Quaker, and these friends of the coloured man help them on their journey northwards, until they are out of the reach of danger.

Our untiring friends, the abolitionists, once obtained a law that no coloured person should be seized as a slave within the free states; this law would have been of great service to us, by ridding us of all anxiety about our freedom while we remained there; but I am sorry to say, that it has lately been repealed, and that now, as before, any coloured person who is said to be a slave, may be seized in the free states and carried away, no matter how long he may have resided there, as also may his children and their children, although they all may have been born there. I hope this law will soon be altered again. At present, many escaped slaves are forwarded by their friends to Canada where, under British rule, they are quite safe. There is a body of ten thousand of them in Upper Canada; they are known for their good order, and loyalty to the British government; during the late troubles, they could always be relied on for the defence of the British possessions, against the lawless Americans who attempted to invade them.

As to the settlement of Liberia on the coast of Africa, the free coloured people of America do not willingly go to it. America is their home: if their forefathers lived in Africa, they themselves know nothing of that country None but free coloured people are taken there: if they would take slaves, they might have plenty of colonists. Slaves will go any where for freedom.

We look very much to Great Britain and Ireland for help. Whenever we hear of the British or Irish people doing good to black men, we are delighted, and run to tell each other the news. Our kind friends, the abolitionists, are very much encouraged when they hear of meetings and speeches in England in our cause. The first of August, the day when the slaves in the West Indies were made free, is always kept as a day of rejoicing by the American coloured free people.

I do hope and believe that the cause of freedom to the blacks is becoming stronger and stronger every day. I pray for the time to come when freedom shall be established all over the world. Then will men love as brethren; they will delight to do good to one another; and they will thankfully worship the Father of all.

And now I have only to repeat my hearty thanks to all who have done any thing towards obtaining liberty for my coloured brethren, and especially to express my gratitude to those who have helped me to procure for myself, my wife, and some of my children, the blessing of freedom, -- a blessing of which none can know the value but he who has been a slave. Whatever profit may be obtained by the sale of this book, and all donations with which I may be favoured, will be faithfully employed in redeeming my remaining children and relatives from the dreadful condition of slavery. Mr. Scoble, the Secretary of the British and Foreign Anti-slavery Society, has kindly agreed to take charge of whatever money I may be able to raise; and any reference may be made to Mr. Rouse at the office of the above Society, 27, New Broad Street, London; or to Mr. R. D. Webb, 160, Great Brunswick Street, Dublin.

DUBLIN, PRINTED BY WEBB AND CHAPMAN,
GREAT BRUNSWICK-ST.

<u>Author's Note</u>:   There was a second printing of the narrative in Boston, Massachusetts in the year 1844. The title of the book is *Narrative of the Life of Moses Grandy, Formerly A Slave in the United States of America*. A gentleman named Oliver Johnson was the publisher. The purpose of the book was to be "sold for the benefit of his relations still in slavery". It also provides the sums of money Moses spent to redeem himself and relatives from slavery. As of January 19, 1844, Moses Grandy had spent $3,060 to redeem himself, wife, son, grandchild, and redeem his kidnapped son. He was also trying to buy the freedom of one of his sisters in Elizabeth City, NC for the sum of $100.00.

To give you an idea of how much that would be in current year dollars, I contacted the Bureau of Labor Statistics at the U.S. Department of Labor to get the formula and assistance for calculating this effort. The United States City Average Consumer Price Index for May 2003 was 549.7. The sum of money Moses Grandy paid for the redemption of his family is equivalent to us spending $52,565.06 in today's economy. I would speculate that the majority of us living in this modern day era of wealth in the United States of America would find this one accomplishment by Moses Grandy alone worthy of recognition and honor.

Just think, if you had to buy your relatives and you needed to come up with $52, 000.00! Could you do so? I do not think it would be easy for most of us. Nor do I think many U.S. citizens would be able to accomplish this noble cause in today's economy without major financial adjustments.

This is a simple comparison of the two different historical eras to measure the impact of what Moses Grandy did in his day. As we look for role models of future generations, let us make sure we have recognized and honored the unsung role models of the past.

The old Courthouse/Jail Museum in Camden County.

A display recognizing Moses Grandy on the second floor of the old Courthouse Jail/Museum.

The historic Camden County Jail/Museum
Built 1910 – Restored 1986

Chapter 3

THE SLAVE NARRATIVE COMMENTARY

Now that you have read the narrative, I hope that it touched you in a way that makes you re-evaluate your outlook on slavery and America's slave history. The affects of slavery on the descendants of slaves are more personal to me now. American slavery has been skimmed over in our history books and public school systems. If the history books do not tell the truth in a manner that satisfies your need for a complete and accurate accounting of your past, then it is up to us to research and write the books.

My objective in this chapter is to provide some interesting points of information on some of the individuals and places mentioned in the narrative, and some of my relatives still living in Camden, North Carolina.

Some of the names mentioned in the *Introduction* chapter of the narrative should be household names in our communities, with the recognition and honor bestowed to individuals and organizations that contributed so greatly to the process of liberating human beings from the agonizing horrors of slavery. Why are they not household names? Maybe that is a question for all the so-called Talented 10th of the African-American community. I won't wait for the answer.

I do not believe that Moses Grandy or some of the other more recognizable names of freedom fighters in this era of American history were the only participants in the quest for freedom. We should research the history of our own relatives and ancestors to include the rich history and legacy of these pioneers of labor that literally built this country. Their stories must be told in order to honor them and prevent such atrocities from ever touching the shores of this country again.

It is our responsibility as Americans to uncover the facts and identify the fiction in our slave history. We must give our future generations a true picture of the courage, sacrifices, and faith displayed by our ancestors, both black and white, that endured the hardships of this turbulent society. I am a firm believer that the truth will set us free.

I have a theory that history can be used as a positive force of information to heal us and become a truly united nation. No longer shall we be indifferent to our past, as if we would like it to be cast off into space. The research for this book opened my eyes to many historical facts that I did not know before pursuing this effort.

The stories of others can provide the medicine necessary to heal this nation and should be brought to the forefront of our consciousness for its redemptive values. The events of September 11, 2001, further illustrate the urgency of the need to heal our nation. Together we suffered the pains of the deaths of so many innocent people. I have never witnessed the coming together of Americans on such a large scale as a result of that one catastrophic event. Like 9/11, we as a nation must also share the pain and triumphs of our slavery history.

I had been looking into the Grandy side of my family history for about a year, and in December 2000 I decided to take my family to Elizabeth City, North Carolina and visit my mother-in-law, as we have done on many occasions. However, this particular time I remembered that my father told me he was born in a place called Fentress, Virginia (now Chesapeake, Virginia) which is on the way to Elizabeth City. I had never been there, but I was given some information from a cousin in Baltimore that I could use to eventually contact other cousins in Chesapeake.

One of my cousins in Chesapeake, whose last name is Grandy, was very cooperative and gave me information on other relatives living in the area. I asked him where was the family cemetery so I could get genealogy information from the headstones. He told me that older family members were not buried in Chesapeake, Virginia, but in the church cemetery in North Carolina.

Of course this was news to me because at that point I did not know there was a North Carolina connection for the Grandys. I asked him what was the name of the church and in what town was it was located. He replied, "New Sawyer's Creek Baptist Church in Camden, North Carolina." Later that day after arriving in Elizabeth City, I asked my mother-in-law for directions to the church.

I decided to visit New Sawyers Creek Baptist Church the next day, which was Sunday. I was able to attend service and introduced myself to the congregation. After service, I met a few of the members who showed me some of the graves where my relatives were buried and suggested that I talk to the church mother who is the oldest living female member of the church.

I wrote on the church program the dates of birth and death (1827-1906) of my great-great grandfather, Edmond Grandy. He was born around the same year Moses Grandy got his free papers. I then returned to meet the church mother, Mrs. Golena Hughes. It was a blessing to meet someone who was, at that time, ninety years old and whose memory was still crystal clear. The first thing she did was to inform me that we were indeed related.

On subsequent visits to the North Carolina she took me on a tour of Camden and the town of Belcross. She showed me some interesting sites that included the yard in which she and my grandmother played in as children when my grandmother would visit them from Fentress, Virginia. I was excited and encouraged by all the new information I was receiving. At that time, my objective was to go back as far as I could on the Grandy research and hoped that it would lead to tracing my African ancestry to a particular country in Africa.

Once I returned home, I continued looking for leads for my research. Months later I did a word search on the computer for a place I had seen on a North Carolina map called Grandy, North Carolina, thinking that might be a link to the family research I was doing. Well, I did not get what I *wanted* on the word search for Grandy, North Carolina. Instead, I got exactly what I *needed* from the word search on the computer.

Headstone and grave of Edmond Grandy, my great-great grandfather, June 4, 1827- April 28, 1906.

New Sawyer's Creek Missionary Baptist Church of Camden, North Carolina founded in 1866.

In March 2001, I came upon the electronic edition of the University of North Carolina at Chapel Hill Libraries, *"Documenting the American South"* Collection, *"Narrative of the Life of Moses Grandy, Late a Slave in the United States of America"*.

I visited the campus library and was able to read from one of the original books published in 1843 that resides in the University's collection. Touching that wealth of information written and published in a document almost 160 years ago gave me a sense of being directly linked to the people in the past that worked so diligently and at great risk to make this book a reality.

My Grandy genealogy research is not complete, nor is the mission that Moses Grandy undertook from the beginning completed. He got it started and I am continuing the effort. Hopefully, this chapter has provided insight into the journey I have traveled thus far in my research. I do not want to make this journey by myself. We owe our ancestors the respect of finding them. The timing is now and they are calling us.

However, let me emphasize and clearly state that this book is not a scientific or technical project on genealogy research. This book is about real people and their struggles to find freedom and liberty. There is no amount of research I can do that would let me know how our enslaved ancestors felt within their souls. I can only imagine the kind of suffering that took place that would endear them to embrace the thought of being struck by lightning as a blessing from God to deliver them from slavery.

These treasures of our oral and documented history should be embraced as legacies of the African-American story and the story of all America. Moses Grandy was blessed to have his story documented for generations of people to study and learn.

I am sure many similar stories have been told and passed down through families without the benefit of having them documented. They are all our ancestors regardless of how we feel and it's time they are treated as such. This book is one way in which the process begins with my family and me.

Chapter 4

BEYOND THE NARRATIVE

Although my research on the Grandy side of my family is far from complete, I believe devoting a chapter on some interesting highlights I discovered relative to Moses and the narrative would be fascinating reading.

I know many of you want to know what became of Moses Grandy. Well, the truth is I have not uncovered that critical piece of this most intriguing puzzle yet. But, I am sure that through the efforts of researchers, scholars, and his relatives, we will make every effort to make the puzzle complete.

I have listed what I consider some of the most interesting discoveries on this genealogical journey to this point. I could list many more but my intention for writing this book is to share some of the information I researched and encourage others to get started on their own research.

1. Moses Grandy had a son named Thomas F. Grandy. In August 1842 they signed up as seamen to board a ship from Boston. Thomas was fifteen years old at the time, which makes him the same age as my great-great grandfather

Edmond Grandy. Edmond named one of his sons Thomas. My great grandfather was named Thomas and so was my grandmother's brother. This could be a coincidence but it may not be. Many slaves would keep the same given names in the family if at all possible to provide a way of tracing lost relatives if they were sold off to other plantations.

2. Moses Grandy was married twice to women who were owned by Enoch Sawyer. I have met some of the African-American Sawyers of Camden County and hope they will share the stories and information from their history.

3. Willie McPherson of Camden County died in December 1835 at the Eagle Hotel in Norfolk, Virginia. He was considered one of the wealthiest men in Camden County at the time of his death.

4. The commissioners authorized the original Camden County Courthouse for construction in 1782. The original courthouse was replaced in 1847 with the current structure. The courthouse was a central location for activities in the county in those days.

In the narrative, Moses said the courthouse was about a mile from where he was so he could get there before Enoch Sawyer could hire him as a young man. The Federal census lists that area as the Camden County Courthouse Township. My ancestors were born and buried in the same township.

5. Enoch Sawyer was the older brother of Lemuel Sawyer who was a member of Congress representing the state of North Carolina. The Autobiography of Lemuel Sawyer corroborates some of the geographical and personal references in the Moses Grandy slave narrative.

6. The 1844 Boston edition of the slave narrative listed the sums of money he spent to redeem himself and family members from slavery. For his own freedom he paid $1,850. For his wife he paid $300, his son $450, grandchild $400, and $60 to redeem his kidnapped son. I asked the Bureau of Labor and Statistics for assistance in calculating how much money would that would be in today's dollars. Taking into account the consumer price index (CPI) from 1830 and May 2003, the total amount Moses paid in today's dollars would be $52,565.06.

7. The Great Dismal Swamp Canal was started in 1793 and built by slave labor in very harsh conditions, as elaborated by Moses in the narrative. The important and significant role the

canal played when the British proceeded with a blockade of the Atlantic Ocean is a critical moment in our history. The canal enabled military to move supplies between Norfolk and Elizabeth City and contributed to the security of this nation.

8. I visited the African Meeting House in Boston, Massachusetts where Moses attended meetings and met with some of the Anti-Slavery Society members of that day. The Boston City Directory of the 1830's listed Moses Grandy and his addresses.

9. The Old Camden County Jail, that is located next to the courthouse, has been restored and the second floor is now a museum. While visiting there in August 2002, I observed an exhibit they have for Moses Grandy. It was a single page document that made reference to his narrative.

10. The University of Montreal in Canada published a French edition of the slave narrative in 1976.

By highlighting these ten interesting facts, it does not mean that I have finished my quest for tracing my Grandy roots. It is only a snapshot in time of my progress to date. I look forward to sharing the full scope of my continuing research in public speaking engagements and/or additional writing projects.

The current Camden County Courthouse, circa 1857. The courthouse is currently under construction renovations.

Historical sign on Route 158 in Camden County recognizing Lemuel Sawyer, a member of the U.S. Congress and author of "Blackbeard, a Comedy" in 1824. He was also the brother of Enoch Sawyer, former slave master of Moses Grandy.

Chapter 5

PEOPLE, PLACES AND THINGS

There are so many significant pieces of historical information that I discovered from reading and researching the narrative. I will only address the topics in this chapter that I believe provide a basis for continuation of my genealogy research, or topics that seem to have historically relevant issues that could result in potentially value added information for embracing our unique and proud African-American heritage.

I think it is also important to discuss some of the individuals mentioned in the narrative. I have collected information about some of these individuals from various public database sources that help shed light on the culture at that time and provide lessons that may be of some relevance in our society today.

Undertaking this journey has been both rewarding and exciting. I have gotten so much pleasure out of meeting people, visiting places, and learning new things about my ancestry that I have become an advocate of researching our family histories and hope to see more of us pursue this type of research. Reading about my research journey may provide hints or ideas on conducting your own family research.

Although I still have a tremendous amount of Grandy ancestral research to accomplish, I believe what I have already completed can help others get started. The key word here is "started". Once you decide that genealogy research is something you want to do, by all means get the ball rolling with yourself or other relatives that can help in the process. Partners can always try to keep each other motivated to reach their desired goals.

More often than not, it seems as though the best place to start is at the beginning. In this case I am going to follow that rule of thumb and start with the cover page of the narrative.

The narrative was originally published in London, England in 1843. However, there was also a Boston edition that was published in 1844, which had some minor changes. The most notable change to the Boston edition was the last page. The Boston edition deleted the London edition's specific request that any funds obtained from the book sale be used to help Moses Grandy redeem his relatives still held in captivity in the United States. However, the Boston edition did list the amounts of money Moses paid for family members he had redeemed from slavery at that time.

The British and Foreign Anti-Slavery Society (now known as Anti-Slavery International) contributed greatly to the freedom fight for slaves then and even today. The individuals that made Moses Grandy's narrative a reality were associated with The British and Foreign Anti-Slavery Society. The names of George Thompson, Charles Gilpin, Thomas Clarkson, Webb and Chapman Printers, John Scoble, and many others from Europe were instrumental in carrying forth the societies significant and heroic efforts to eradicate slavery in the United States.

Some other notable Americans were mentioned in the narrative introduction. They included such people as William Lloyd Garrison, Nathan Winslow, Samuel Sewall, and many others whose names and memories should be etched in the pages of African-American history books.

This genealogical journey allowed me to travel and meet relatives in Camden, North Carolina on several occasions to do research. Of course it helped to have a mother-in-law that lived in Elizabeth City, North Carolina, which is a fifteen minutes from the Courthouse Township of Camden, where the majority of the narrative's story takes place.

I was very fortunate to have two relatives who lived in the area and paved the way for me to get connected in the community. First, my mother-in law, Dorothy

Welch Robinson, grew up in Elizabeth City and attended Elizabeth City State Teachers College (now Elizabeth City State University). Second, the New Sawyer's Creek Baptist Church member my ninety-three year-old cousin, Ms. Golena Hughes, was raised in Camden County and now lives in Elizabeth City.

Through these two wonderful women, I was able to save valuable time in becoming familiar with the area and meeting the people.

As it turns out, I seem to be related to many of the black residents still living in the Camden County Courthouse Township. The Register of Deeds Office at the Camden County Courthouse was very helpful in assisting me with researching birth, death, and marriage certificates of my relatives.

As I searched through many documents in Camden County Courthouse and the North Carolina State Archives in Raleigh, North Carolina, I was astonished to see the many surnames of individuals mentioned in the narrative show up on census documents, deeds, wills and other legal documents. It brought on a feeling of actually traveling back in time to the late 1700s and early 1800s.

Another source of valuable information became available when I joined the local historical society. These organizations can provide valuable information on the history of the towns and past local residents. I have met many other researchers in various places that provided me with suggestions on conducting my research and who shared some of their experiences.

These new friendships and memories gained on this journey will be treasured forever. This has indeed been an experience that I encourage, and hopefully through this book, inspire others to take. Some of your family history may be related to mine. We will never know unless you take the journey for yourself. The ancestors are calling us to tell their story. Will you answer the call?

Mrs. Golena Hughes of Elizabeth City, North Carolina. Cousin Golena was my tour guide for research in Camden County.

Pictures of Willoughby Spence and Lillian Grandy Spence. They raised Cousin Golena Hughes and her siblings in Camden, North Carolina after the death of their mother.

Ms. Ann Sawyer and staff at the Camden, North Carolina Register of Deeds Office.

Register of Deeds Office in Camden Courthouse.

The Grandy Primary School located in Camden, (NC).

The bridge and waterway between Camden, (NC) and Elizabeth City, (NC).

Chapter 6

RELATIVES AND RELATIONS

The experience of genealogy research has greatly benefited my immediate family and friends. We have met so many wonderful people within the last few years and we are related to many of them. I consider my research a little beyond the infancy stage. I have traveled from Maryland to Massachusetts, Rhode Island, New York, New Orleans, North Carolina, and Virginia. I have met relatives that have received me, in most cases, with open arms. What a journey! And it's not over. I want all of them to know that I truly appreciate the hospitality shown to me. There is still such a tradition called southern hospitality that is alive and well in the Grandy family.

We are descendents of slaves and they were survivors of slavery. In the Moses Grandy slave narrative there is a statement on the front page that states, "published and sold for the benefit of his relations still in slavery". What a role model Moses Grandy was and still is today. What courage and vision he had to plant the seeds of freedom for himself, family, relatives, and other slaves during this era. The Grandy relatives that I have come to know during this research have enriched my life experience tremendously. To meet people for the first time that seem as if you've known them for a lifetime provides encouragement to me for continuing this journey. I have heard from them the stories of some of my relatives that have passed on and some of them still living that span three centuries.

In writing this chapter I wanted to mention a few moments in which I met relatives without going into the genealogical details.

- Many relatives I met at a cookout in Moyock, North Carolina during the summer of 2001. Nothing like an old fashion southern cookout to become acquainted with relatives and the untold stories.
- I met some relatives in Springfield, Massachusetts after going to Boston and Portland, Maine earlier that same day. Although I arrived to my destination late that evening, I was greeted very warmly by my cousins and given a delicious meal to welcome me.
- My father and several older cousins from Baltimore, Maryland provided me with insight of how I was related to cousins in Chesapeake and Virginia Beach, Virginia.
- Relatives in Chesapeake, Virginia and Elizabeth City, North Carolina provided information on history, relatives, and places in Camden, North Carolina that no amount of documentation gathered through genealogical research could come close to providing. I am truly blessed to

have had them assist me with insightful information.

With much gratitude I thank them all for their support and encouragement.

To enable family members and friends to recognize some of the extended relatives, I have included Appendices A, B, C and D on marriages by people with the surname of Grandy to other families in Norfolk County, Virginia, City of Norfolk, Virginia and Camden County, North Carolina. I hope that this information can be used to bring relatives and extended family and friends together again.

I do not want to just "build" a family tree, but also to use the lumber from the trees to build a mansion. My hope is that in some way I am continuing the efforts of Moses Grandy in laying a foundation to build upon.

Great-great Aunt Learah Grandy Cartwright, sister of my great grandfather, Thomas Grandy.

Chapter 7

LABOR PIONEERS

Through my extensive family research, I have reached a conclusion in my mind about who rightfully deserves the recognition for Labor Day in America; the former African-American slaves.

Our slave ancestors built a significant portion of this country. That is an undisputed fact. This is a fact that people of African ancestry in this country, including myself, need to take more seriously. If we do not give them the recognition they deserve, then who will? This country may not be proud of its slave history, but we should be proud of those slaves that survived and those that did not survive this horrific time in our country's history.

We must find positive ways to honor their memory. Today we celebrate Labor Day as a day of rest from our work life. It means much more to me after doing this research on my family. To see headstones of my ancestors from the 1800's in Camden, North Carolina and walk the land where they were held as captives was enough to change my perspective on what Labor Day in America means to me.

The reality of their struggles and spiritual strength becomes clearer for me by visiting the land my ancestors came from. I get a renewed sense of strength, focus, determination, and spirit from being there. Will this small token of recognition impact or change African American social or economic status in America? I do not know. But, we have to start somewhere and do something positive to impact the continuing struggle for total liberation, justice and righteousness.

The Three Phases of Freedom

I think there are three phases of freedom that we must go through. The first is **Physical** freedom. This phase of freedom is the removal of chains and laws that held us in captivity. We have for the most part accomplished this phase.

The second phase is **Mental** freedom. This phase deals with the reality and after effects of our slave history. The majority of us are in this phase of freedom. That includes all Americans no matter what their ethnic origin happens to be.

The third and more challenging phase is **Spiritual** freedom. An entire book could be written on this topic alone. Most of us have not scratched the surface on this phase of freedom. We are part of the continuation process of the labor pioneers that went through the physical phase of freedom. We should embrace our responsibilities of being a part of the process that will one day result in Spiritual liberation.

Chapter 8

REACH BACK AND MOVE FORWARD

Getting in touch with your past may help to enhance your future. This is just a theory of mine. I know sometimes it is painful to revisit our ancestors' slavery past. The fact of the matter is they lived through it and they would want us to remember them. We need to build on what they left for us. I mentioned before that this is not just for Grandy slave descendants, but also for slave descendants around the world.

In 2003, we are still living in a world where accounts of the human slave trade still exist. The good news is that organizations such as Anti-Slavery International and Free The Slaves continue to carry the banner of doing what they can to eradicate slavery. Their roots can be traced back to the British and Foreign Anti-Slavery Society that helped Moses Grandy and many other slaves in their quest for freedom.

I have found in my research that many positive stories about black and white families during the American slave era have never gotten the recognition and credit they deserve. Moses Grandy's story is only one of them. What story in your family's history is waiting for you to bring it to the forefront of the American Society?

I gave a short speech earlier this year during a Black History Month luncheon. Afterwards, some people wanted to know how they could get started doing their own genealogy research. They also wanted to know what resources are available to help them conduct genealogy research.

Genealogy research is not my profession, and I am not an expert in this field. But, I must admit I have learned quite a few techniques from the professionals in this area. I find that getting started is one of the most difficult parts of genealogy research.

How to fit research time in with all the other busy aspects of life was the most difficult part for me. Many of us have families, jobs, financial obligations, and so on. Pick any excuse you have and it would be a good one. What keeps me going is the call of my ancestors wanting all of us to remember them. This is not just something I want to do. It is something that I have to do.

For me, this type of research is rewarding and fulfilling. I enjoy helping others to discover their past. I also appreciate the dedicated professionals that work at the record preservation places to preserve our past. The records and documents maintained by these individuals are so important to tracing back the events of our past. I salute their efforts and their assistance to researchers.

Chapter 9

OUR TURN

The time has come for me to make contributions that capture the healing powers of history. The information gathered from researching history has the power to heal or hurt. I choose healing history. I believe things happen for a reason and my efforts to research and write this book is not an accident. The University of North Carolina at Chapel Hill Libraries deserves credit for digitizing the slave narratives and other documents of the antebellum era. They invited me to participate in their *Documenting The American South* 1000th Document Celebration.

This event plus many other instances of spiritual awakening moments during this journey allowed me to focus some of my energies in the direction of what history has to tell us that could yield benefits for our future generations.

Most important to me was the revelation that my ancestry did not start in North Carolina. Nor did it start in the United States. There are thousands of years that seem to be lost in the wind about our history. However, the documents, papers, and oral history have limited lasting power when dealing with the physical and material breakdowns of scientific properties associated with living in this earthly environment.

Our connection to the past must involve the spiritual relationship as stated in Deuteronomy, Chapter 30 of the Torah (first five books of the Old Testament). Some of you may be asking yourself "What does that have to do with me?" My answer is maybe nothing and possibly everything. Is there a connection between the ancient slaves of Egypt and the recent slaves in America?

I don't know about you, but this question intrigues me. It made me look outside the box of religious traditions, brainwashing doctrines, and finger pointing customs to opening the windows of discovering the truth about my ancestors' history. If there is a connection between the Egyptian and American slave histories, I want to know about it. As a matter of fact I have researched it.

The discovery of knowledge and history is well worth the effort. It is a new sense of freedom that stirs my soul. Our history does not end with great-great-great grandmother or grandfather. However, if we can research our history to that point, what a proud accomplishment that would be for most of us.

I may not have all the answers, but I know that I am prepared to ask better questions about my ancestry than before I started this journey. I find myself making comments to my family and friends that seem to shed light on the work yet to be done. I make the comparison that technologically in the last century we went from the horse and buggy to the shuttle.

We need to make that same kind of leap spiritually and historically to ascend to the next level of freedom. This will be the kind of freedom our future generations to come will enjoy, having it better than what we have. Our slave ancestors survived so that we could have better than what they had. We should never forget that or be ashamed of them.

My work and research is not complete by writing this book. It is just beginning. I cannot devote a full time effort to research my ancestry at this time. Like many of us, I have responsibilities and obligations that must be met on a monthly basis. But, I will give my works and research the time that I can.

This journey has been so rewarding to this point I wanted to share it with others. There is nothing like your passion connecting with your purpose. If I have to continue to do this in my spare time, I shall. This spare time effort keeps the challenges of my life in balance. In some ways it seems to make my life burdens just a little more lighter. If it can do this for me, maybe this type of history can have a healing effect for someone else.

To keep me energized as I continue these types of projects, I have devised my five "P" principles for encouragement. They are Prophecy, Purpose, Passion, Power, and Prosperity. I will not elaborate on them now, however, I believe it is important to establish your own criteria for self-motivation.

To back up my words with action, my wife and I have co-founded a non-profit organization called Slave Descendants Freedom Society, Inc. The mission of this organization is to assist individuals and organizations with genealogy research awareness training, developing empowerment initiatives and promoting slave contributions to America recognition programs.

Our goal is to bring honor, recognition and opportunities for healing to the world by never forgetting our slave history and the descendants of slaves never forgetting their ancestors. If you would like to help in our efforts, please contact us at:

Slave Descendants Freedom Society, Inc.
P.O. Box 8046
Elkridge, Maryland 21075
Email: info@slavedescendants.org
Phone: (410) 796-3165/ Fax: (410) 796-2858
Or visit us at our website: www.slavedescendants.org.

May the peace and blessings of Yahweh (God) be with you and your family as you journey to find the ancestral treasures in your heritage.

APPENDICES A, B, C and D

General Index to Marriages for:
Norfolk County, Virginia
Camden County, North Carolina

and

Male Index to Marriages:
City of Norfolk, Virginia

APPENDIX A

General Index to Marriages – Norfolk County
(Female)
July 1, 1850 to December 31, 1935

Date	Bride	Groom
1/4/1866	Margaret Grandy	Oratto Dosier
1/29/1874	Courtney Grandy	Morris Brown
4/5/1883	Christina Grandy	J.A. Williams
4/7/1884	Ida Grandy	William Chappell
8/27/1885	Ellen Grandy	Samuel Green
12/24/1885	Elizabeth Grandy	Lewis Bland
8/26/1886	Victoria Grandy	Jasper Hopper
12/16/1886	Sarah Grandy	Richard Harris
6/25/1888	Mamie Grandy	Elizah Hill
5/5/1894	Sarah Grandy	John Farmer
12/19/1894	Susan Grandy	Willis Griffin
3/16/1895	Estelle Grandy	William Brock
7/25/1896	Mary Grandy	James Lowh
11/3/1896	Anna Grandy	John Wilson
10/17/1900	Lizzie L. Grandy	David Lamb
7/1/1901	Lizzy Grandy	Issac Martin
1/4/1904	Emma Jane Grandy	George Ferebee
1/19/1910	Cora Grandy	Willie Bryant
9/8/1910	Bessie Lee Grandy	Leroy Smith
5/24/1911	Emma Grandy	Floyd Whitmon
7/3/1913	Francis Grandy	Charlie Gregory
12/12/1916	Lydia Grandy	Hamilton Young

Date	Bride	Groom
10/7/1919	Ethel Grandy	Clarence Carter
12/8/1919	Malinda Grandy	Edward Wynn
6/20//1920	Viola Grandy	Thomas Roni
1/2/1922	Hattie Grandy	John Eyler
8/21/1922	Ellen Grandy	Willie Williams
9/2/1923	Mary Grandy	J. Herman Jackson
8/30/1926	Hattie Grandy	Belton Douglas
4/8/1928	Elnora Grandy	Richard Sheppard
10/25/1934	Annie Grandy	John Harris
10/29/1934	Lillie Grandy	Jessie Jarvis

Note: Partial data gathered from the Norfolk County Courthouse in Chesapeake, Virginia.

APPENDIX B

General Index to Marriages – Norfolk County (Male)
July 1, 1850 to December 31, 1935

Date	Groom	Bride
11/29/1865	Caleb L. Grandy	Burnice Honbury
1/13/1870	Stephen Grandy	Ida Smith
1/18/1877	George W. Grandy	Priscilla Etheridge
5/30/1889	George Grandy	Medora Gibbs
3/19/1893	Charles E. Grandy	Malissa Jackson
7/22/1899	Issac Grandy	Emma Tyler
1/21/1900	Mark Grandy	Corianna Howell
11/26/1901	Dennis Grandy	Lelice Ann Harris
12/24/1903	Emanuel Grandy	Annie Brown
3/7/1906	Alpheus Grandy	Annie Williams
5/10/1906	Henry Grandy	Fannie Jones
11/22/1909	John Thomas Grandy	Rosetta Williams
12/30/1909	Josephus Grandy	Lula Brown
12/3/1913	George Bell Grandy	Elizabeth Dough
4/29/1915	Bill Grandy	Eva Ferebee
11/15/1919	Alfred Grandy	Annie Perry
12/2/1919	George Grandy	Mary Tynes
7/11/1920	George E. Grandy	Georgia Ferebee
10/24/1920	Richard Grandy	Ruth Jackson
9/16/1923	Charles Grandy	Emeline Sawyer
10/11/1924	Rayfield Grandy	Carrie Lee Bowe
6/17/1926	Albert Grandy	Rebecca Jones

APPENDIX B (continued)

Date	Groom	Bride
9/7/1932	William Grandy	Flossie Jones
11/20/1932	Joseph Grandy	Vivian Lawrence
7/19/1933	Henry Grandy	Eliza Eason

Note: Partial data gathered from the Norfolk County Courthouse in Chesapeake, Virginia.

APPENDIX C

General Index to Marriages – Camden County, NC
(Mixed Males and Female)
Beginning thru June 30, 1941

Date	Groom	Bride
7/20/1862	Abner Grandy	Jane Morrisette
8/15/1869	Abner W. Grandy	Permelia Trafton
9/14/1891	Timothy Bowe	Alice Grandy
12/24/1891	Thomas Dozier	Angelica Grandy
11/19/1903	Ambrose Williams	Annie Grandy
3/27/1937	Bryan Grandy	Mamie Ferebee
9/30/1900	C.L. Grandy	Mary E. Garrett
6/29/1898	C.R. Grandy	G.L. Bland
2/13/1881	Aaron Barco	Caroline Grandy
1/12/1888	Charles Grandy	Georgianna Jones
4/25/1872	Lemuel Walston	Cherry Grandy
10/16/1901	Christopher Grandy	Alice Polk
3/17/1882	John Wilson	Claricy Grandy
4/7/1867	Dempsey Grandy	Adeline Harrison
9/24/1937	Roy Mastraco	Dollie Grandy
8/3/1902	Ed Grandy	Hager Lamb
2/18/1872	Aldustus Perkins	Eliza Grandy
6/13/1853	Isaac Forbes	Elizabeth Grandy
1/28/1875	Jackson Sears	Florence Grandy
12/23/1915	Frank Grandy	Martha Hunter
11/16/1848	G.G. Grandy	Martha Homer
9/15/1878	George Grandy	Angeline Gallop

APPENDIX C (continued)

Date	Groom	Bride
4/12/1931	Floyd Gilden	Hazel Grandy
10/25/1900	Will Perkins	Ida Grandy
1/7/1904	Isaac Grandy	Dora Sawyer
2/22/1872	James Grandy	Harriett Duke
12/11/1871	Demsey Lamb	Jane Grandy
11/29/1902	George Sanderlin	Josephine Grandy
9/7/1882	Samuel Williams	Josephine Grandy
1/18/1881	Oscar D. Cartwright	Leah Grandy
11/20/1907	Willie A. Spence	Lillie M. Grandy
1/23/1865	F.R. Jennings	Lizzie Grandy
5/11/1858	M.M. Grandy	M. Sawyer
2/2/1888	Charles Barnard	Mamie Grandy
8/7/1882	Westly Hunter	Margaret Grandy
8/11/1937	Mark C. Grandy	Bernice Herndon
12/17/1885	William Trafton	Mary Ellen Grandy
8/1/1859	Nathan Grandy	Mary Taylor
12/27/1870	Prince Grandy	Francis Humphries
7/30/1905	William Richardson	Sarah Grandy
10/4/1851	James Barrows	Sarah Grandy
5/10/1883	Wilson Jones	Sarah Grandy
2/20/1857	Thos J. Etheridge	Sarah P. Grandy
5/25/1851	Noah Forbes	Susan Grandy

APPENDIX C (continued)

Date	Groom	Bride
3/29/1917	I.H.B. Lowe	Susan M. Grandy
9/14/1871	Thomas Grandy	Casan Cartwright
4/15/1886	Thomas Grandy	Katie Hughes
7/20/1887	Thomas Grandy	Mariah Spence
9/15/1858	W. Hambury	Virginia Grandy
5/28/1938	Wiley Grandy	Mary Griffin
2/20/1875	Willis Grandy	Mandy Shears
6/7/1855	Willis S. Grandy	Sarah Lamb

Note: Partial data gathered from the Camden County Courthouse in Camden, North Carolina.

APPENDIX D

Male Index to Marriages – City of Norfolk, VA

Date	Groom	Bride
10/21/1868	Cyrus Grandy	Mary Selden
7/12/1872	Charles Grandy	Otelia Braxton
2/4/1874	John Grandy	Annie Rowland
6/3/1879	Albert H. Grandy	Annie W. Reid
12/18/1879	Charles Grandy	Eliza Gordon
1/5/1882	Felix G. Grandy	Mary Cartwright
7/24/1883	Frank L. Grandy	Fanny S. Cook
1/19/1888	Henry Grandy	Annie Loach
9/12/1889	Henry Grandy	Sarah Ashley
12/16/1901	George Grandy	Elnora Wilson
4/8/1903	Matthews Grandy	Amanda Keeling
10/4/1904	Thomas L. Grandy	Mary E. Langley
2/20/1905	Miles Grandy	Mary Simons
4/30/1905	Willis Grandy	Mary Minton
8/20/1907	C.W. Grandy	Hattie Perkins
4/26/1911	William J. Grandy	Helen H. Hudgins
5/19/1911	Harry M. Grandy	Bertha L. Smith
9/18/1912	John W. Grandy	Lottie Lambert
5/29/1913	Edward Grandy	Jennie Cherry
11/22/1915	Cecil Grandy	Maggie Saulsberry
6/12/1916	Sam Grandy	Mary Johnson
9/27/1916	Alfred Grandy	Rosa Coplin
12/4/1916	Morris H. Grandy	Mary E. Brown
1/27/1920	John T. Grandy	Lurola Brown
11/11/1920	Robert Grandy	Josephine Christian

9/3/1926	Robert E. Grandy	Anna M. Saunders
6/27/1929	William B. Grandy	Selena Jones
6/1/1935	Willie E. Grandy	Alberta Stokley
2/4/1936	William J. Grandy	Mary L. Hickman
11/23/1936	Abbott Grandy	Maggie Jones
12/8/1936	George Grandy	Cornelia Johnson
5/29/1937	Jessie Grandy	Josephine Edwards
12/27/1938	John Grandy	Louise Mclese
10/19/1942	John W. Grandy III	Anne R. Evans
4/12/1944	Melvin Grandy	Hattie Champion
5/21/1946	Robert N. Grandy	Jean C. Bell
8/2/1947	Joseph Grandy	Doris Sykes
7/1/1950	Clifford G. Grandy	Ida M. Rogers
2/12/1951	Charles F. Grandy	Miriam W. King
12/14/1951	Joseph J. Grandy	Margie McNeil
10/18/1954	Henry Grandy	Gladys F. Gallop
6/24/1955	Charles C. Grandy	Sarah F. Sivels
3/31/1958	Joseph J. Grandy	Dorothy Williams
6/15/1959	Clinton L. Grandy	Audrey McNair
6/28/1977	Joseph Grandy Sr.	Virginia Porter
11/10/1983	Cyros W. Grandy	Edith Holcombe

Note: Partial data gathered from the City of Norfolk courthouse in Norfolk, Virginia.

Ancestor's Call
Book Order Form

Send form and payment to:
Tech-Rep Associates, Inc., P.O. Box 8046
Elkridge, Maryland 21075

Name_____

Address_____

City_____ State_____ Zip_____

Ph.#_____Email_____

# of copies_____x$12.95 =Total Cost $_____
Sales Tax (MD 5%) $_____
*Shipping & Handling $____3.00_____
Total Due $_____

* For all orders over 2 books or international orders, please call for shipping charges.

Method of Payment (Please check one):
Check _____ Money Order_____

Visa_____ MasterCard_____
(Please make payable to: **Tech-Rep Associates, Inc.**)

Card #: _____ Exp Date_____

Authorization Signature:

_____